The Usborne
Little Book
of
Chocolate

First published in 2010 by Usborne Publishing Ltd.,
Usborne House, 83-85 Saffron Hill, London, ECIN 8RT, England
www.usborne.com

The Usborne
Little Book
of
Chocolate

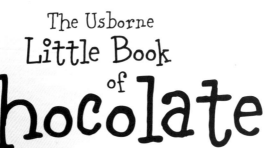

Sarah Khan

Designed by Kate Rimmer

Illustrated by Stephen Lambert

Digital manipulation by Keith Furnival

Consultant: Amelia Rope

Edited by Kirsteen Rogers

Usborne Quicklinks

The Usborne Quicklinks Website is packed with thousands of links to all the best websites on the internet. The websites include information, video clips, sounds, games and animations that support and enhance the information in Usborne internet-linked books.

To visit the recommended websites for the *Little Book of Chocolate*, go to the Usborne Quicklinks Website at **www.usborne-quicklinks.com** and enter the keywords: **little chocolate**

Internet safety

When using the internet please follow the internet safety guidelines displayed on the Usborne Quicklinks Website. The websites recommended at Usborne Quicklinks are regularly reviewed. However, the content of a website may change at any time and Usborne Publishing is not responsible for the content of websites other than its own. We recommend that children are supervised while on the internet.

Contents

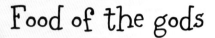

Food of the gods

Chocolate can be milk or dark, sweet or bitter, an expensive luxury or a cheap snack. But, whatever the type of chocolate, it all comes from trees. The tree's scientific name, *Theobroma cacao*, means "food of the gods" in Greek, and to many chocolate-lovers, chocolate is exactly that. Cacao trees grow fruit, called pods. Inside the pods are seeds, which are also known as beans. From these beans come cocoa powder and cocoa butter, which combine to make chocolate.

This glossy, smooth chocolate sauce began as a pile of dry, bitter cacao seeds.

The top 10 countries that grow the most cacao are:

1 – Ivory Coast
2 – Ghana
3 – Indonesia
4 – Nigeria
5 – Brazil
6 – Cameroon
7 – Ecuador
8 – Dominican Republic
9 – Papua New Guinea
10 – Malaysia

Where chocolate comes from

Cacao trees grow in hot, rainy areas. There are cacao plantations all over South America, West Africa, Asia and the Caribbean. The Ivory Coast, in West Africa, is the biggest grower of cacao, producing enough to make over a third of the world's chocolate. There are huge chocolate factories all over the world, but the biggest one is in Pennsylvania, USA.

Supernatural and super-rich

Throughout history, chocolate has been an important and special food. Over 2,000 years ago, Mexican people told stories of a feathered god who angered the other deities by teaching humans how to make the drink of the gods – liquid chocolate.

Ancient Mexicans carved images of cacao and the god Quetzalcoatl into palace and temple walls.

Even when chocolate reached Europe around 500 years ago, only the very wealthy could afford it. Today, chocolate is much more accessible, and is sold in shops all over the world. But the very best quality, gourmet chocolates are still a luxury.

These luxury chocolates are made with the highest-quality ingredients, which pushes up their price.

One of the world's most expensive chocolates is a dark truffle sold in a gourmet chocolate shop in Connecticut, USA. Each truffle costs $250.

Delicious discovery

No one really knows how chocolate was discovered. Historians think that the first people to make it were the Olmec people, who lived in Mexico around 3,000 years ago. The Olmecs may have seen animals eating the sweet flesh of cacao pods, but then spitting out the beans because of their bitter taste.

South American monkeys feast on the fruit of cacao trees.

The white, sticky stuff inside this cacao pod is the edible flesh which surrounds the beans.

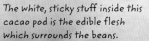

From bean to chocolate

How the Olmecs first realized that bitter cacao beans could be made into a tasty treat is a bit of a mystery. To do so, they had to scoop the beans out of the pod, leave them to ferment until they turned dark brown, dry them in the hot sun, roast them over a fire, grind them into a thick paste, then mix them with water.

The Olmecs covered the beans with banana leaves, and left them to ferment for a few days.

A bitter drink

Solid chocolate wasn't invented until 1674 so, for most of its history, chocolate has just been enjoyed as a drink. The chocolate that the Olmecs sipped was very different from the hot, chocolatey drinks we have today. Their chocolate was spicy and bitter, and was served cold.

The Olmecs added herbs, spices and chillies to the chocolate paste.

Growing cacao

Not keen on trekking into the rainforest every time they wanted to make some more chocolate, the Olmecs decided to grow the trees in their own fields. They found that the trees weren't easy to look after – cacao can't grow in places that are too high, too cold, or too dry, and they need shelter from wind and sun. But the Olmecs found ways to provide the trees with everything they needed to flourish.

As well as turning cacao beans into a drinking chocolate, the Olmecs also used the flesh of cacao pods to make a strong alcoholic drink.

Cacao trees need shade, so the Olmecs planted them near the edge of rainforests, next to taller trees.

Magic beans

From around 250AD right up until the 1500s, there were large groups of people in Central and South America whose societies "ran" on chocolate. The Mayan people and, later on, the Aztecs believed that cacao beans were magical, or even holy, and used them in rituals of birth, marriage and death. They also used cacao beans as money.

Hot or cold

Both the Mayans and the Aztecs drank chocolate, but the Mayans drank it hot while the Aztecs preferred it cold. In Mayan society, everyone – no matter how poor they were – could occasionally enjoy a chocolate drink. Before drinking it, they poured it back and forth between a cup and a pot until a thick foam frothed up on top.

Mayans liked chocolate froth so much they even poured it over other, corn-based drinks.

Buying beans

By the 1400s, the Aztecs had taken over as the most powerful civilization in Central and South America. Cacao became very important to the Aztecs – not only as a luxury drink, but also as money, offerings to their gods, and taxes paid to rulers.

Cacao beans were very valuable in the Aztec world. This was because the Aztecs were based in the dry highlands of central Mexico where cacao trees couldn't grow, so they had to buy the beans by trading with people in cacao-growing regions.

Fit for a king

Chocolate was the champagne and caviar of the Aztec world in that only the richest and most important people could afford to have it. Emperor Montezuma II, ruler of the Aztecs in the early 1500s, is said to have drunk 50 cups every day, served in solid gold goblets that were thrown away after one use.

The Aztecs thought that chocolate was the blood of the Earth. Their emperors drank chocolate that was dyed with seeds from annatto trees, to make it blood-red.

An Aztec price list:

1 turkey rooster – 300 beans

1 turkey hen – 100 beans

1 slave – 100 beans

1 small rabbit – 30 beans

1 cup of chocolate made from 8 beans

1 avocado – 3 beans

1 large tomato – 1 bean

A medical marvel

In 1519, a Spanish explorer named Hernán Cortés arrived in Mexico and met the Emperor of the Aztecs. At the meeting, Cortés was given chocolate to drink. Over time, he came to realize that cacao beans could make him rich. During the next few years, the enterprising explorer set up cacao plantations in Mexico, Haiti and Trinidad.

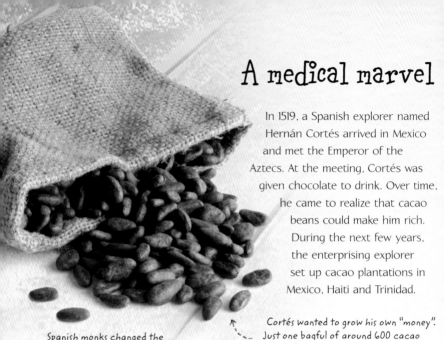

Cortés wanted to grow his own "money". Just one bagful of around 600 cacao beans, like this, could buy him two canoes.

Spanish monks changed the Aztec recipe by removing the chilli, adding nutmeg, and serving the drink warm.

A Spanish secret

In 1544, Mayan nobles visited Spain, bringing chocolate as a gift for the king. Chocolate soon became popular among the aristocracy. They wanted to be the only people outside South and Central America to have the recipe, and only allowed Spanish monks to make chocolate. The monks kept the recipe secret for over a hundred years.

An alternative medicine

The Aztecs believed that drinking chocolate made people stronger and more alert, so when it first came to Spain, aristocrats drank it for its health benefits as well as its taste. Doctors prescribed it to them for curing fevers, helping digestion, and easing pain. The Spanish Catholic Church also allowed them to drink chocolate to keep them going during times of fasting, when they gave up solid foods to help them concentrate on prayer.

Explorer Hernán Cortés wrote that the Aztec Emperor Montezuma saw chocolate as a "divine drink which builds up resistance and fights fatigue. A cup of this precious drink permits man to walk for a whole day without food".

A continental cure

The Spanish couldn't keep chocolate under wraps forever. Some historians think that the secret got out because the Spanish monks shared it with visiting French monks. After reaching France, the secret spread to Italy and then to the rest of Europe.

Doctors kept on adding to the recipe. They mixed the cacao with a variety of herbs, flowers and nuts – the ingredients varied, depending on what illness needed curing. Many doctors also mixed other medicines with chocolate to disguise the horrible taste of the remedies.

In the 1500s, Spanish doctors thought that chocolate was strengthening, so prescribed it to patients who were thin and weak.

Spanish nuns went to Mexico to preach to the natives, and learned chocolate-making.

A sweet treat

In the mid 1500s, Spain took control of Mexico. By this time, the Spanish already governed many Caribbean islands and grew cane sugar there. Now they had cacao and sugar, so combined the two. The first people to mix sugar into chocolate were Spanish nuns in Mexico. Their sweetened recipe made its way back to Spain, where it was an instant hit in the Spanish royal court.

A royal wedding

Princess Maria Theresa

Drinking chocolate became a craze amongst the upper classes in France after their king, Louis XIV, married a Spanish princess, Maria Theresa, in 1660. The princess brought her precious cacao beans over from Spain, as well as her chocolate-loving ladies-in-waiting, and servants to make the drink for her. Sweet, hot chocolate was served at the wedding to the guests, who were the most important people in Europe.

French king, Louis XIV, added an egg yolk to the Spanish hot chocolate recipe to thicken it.

Cacao from the colonies

As chocolate became more and more popular throughout the 1600s, France, Holland and England set up their own cacao plantations in the Caribbean, Asia and Central and South America. Having their own supplies meant that they didn't have to buy cacao from Spain any more.

By the 1600s, drinking chocolate came in the form of cacao cakes, that could be crumbled and mixed with hot water and sugar.

In the shops

In Spain and France, chocolate was the drink of royalty and aristocracy. But, when it reached England and Holland, shopkeepers started to sell the new drink to the public. But it was still very expensive, and only the wealthy could afford to drink it regularly.

Chocolate houses – the chocolate equivalent of coffee shops – began springing up all over England from the mid 1600s. There was an entrance fee, but this didn't put off rich customers, who flocked to the houses to enjoy a hot drink, discuss politics, socialize, and gamble.

For fashionable young Londoners, chocolate houses were the places to be.

Early European chocolate-makers used to crush cacao beans with a rolling pin.

Before mechanical mills were used, chocolate had been gritty, but the mechanical grinding process gave it a much smoother texture.

Chocolate boom

Until the 1700s, European chocolate-makers found it hard to keep up with the demand for their product. Cacao beans were being harvested on the plantations, then shipped to Europe to be ground by hand.

While chocolate was still being made in this way, it was time-consuming and expensive to produce. It wasn't until machines came onto the scene that the mass production of chocolate really took off.

Mechanical mills

In 1776, a Frenchman named Doret invented a water-powered mill to grind cacao beans into a paste. Soon afterwards, another Frenchman, named Dubuisson, designed and built a mill driven by steam. It soon became possible to grind huge amounts of cacao and mass-produce chocolate cheaply and quickly. Now everyone could get a taste of the sweet confection.

Some of the earliest cacao grinding machines crushed the beans under steam-powered rollers.

The chocolate pioneers

Throughout the 1800s, pioneering inventors all over Europe kept on coming up with ways to make chocolate better.

In 1815, Dutch chemist Conrad van Houten added a type of salt to cocoa powder to reduce its bitterness and help it mix better with water.

In 1828, van Houten invented a press to remove some of the fat from cocoa beans so they would make a finer powder.

Solid chocolate, like this, was first made by Joseph Fry.

In 1847, English chocolate-maker Joseph Fry developed a chocolate paste that could be shaped and hardened. The result was the first modern chocolate bar.

In 1875, Swiss food manufacturers Daniel Peter and Henri Nestlé added condensed milk to solid chocolate, inventing milk chocolate.

In 1879, Swiss chocolate-maker Rodolphe Lindt invented a machine to mix chocolate to a smooth consistency.

Henri Nestlé found that adding milk to chocolate made it sweeter and creamier.

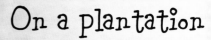

On a plantation

Not all cacao trees are the same. There are three main types: criollos, forasteros and Trinitarios. On a cacao plantation, farmers usually grow a mix of two or three types.

Criollo pods have soft, thin walls and produce the best type of chocolate. They were grown by the Olmecs around 3,000 years ago. Forastero pods are the easiest to cultivate and have thick walls. Trinitarios are a cross between the other two. They are easier to grow than criollos and produce better-tasting chocolate than forasteros.

Around 90% of the world's chocolate comes from forastero cacao pods, like these, because they're the easiest types to grow.

Harvest time

Cacao trees have frail trunks and their roots are shallow, so they would easily be damaged if pod pickers tried to climb them. To reach the pods, pickers snip them off the trees with long-handled steel knives. Pod breakers then split them open to scoop out the beans.

A good breaker can open 500 pods in an hour.

Fermenting

Once the beans have come into contact with the air, they quickly change from beige to a shade of purple. To bring out their chocolatey taste, the beans are piled up and covered. Some farmers cover them with banana leaves, just as the Olmecs used to.

Around the beans is a layer of pulp that starts to heat up and rot, or ferment. The fermenting cacao can reach a temperature up to 50°C (122°F). In about a week, the beans have turned a rich shade of brown, which means they are ready for drying.

Drying out

To stop the beans from fermenting any further, they are dried, either by leaving them out in the sun or by laying them under hot-air pipes. After a few days, when the beans have lost nearly all their moisture and more than half their weight, they're ready to be shipped out to chocolate factories around the world.

Plantation workers shovel the beans into boxes, or throw them into heaps, to ferment.

It takes a single cacao tree one whole year to produce enough beans to make just 450g (1lb) of powdered cocoa.

The best way to dry cacao beans is to spread them onto bamboo mats and let them bake in the sun.

At a chocolate factor

When cacao beans arrive at a chocolate factory, there's still a lot to do to make them into chocolate. First, they're poured into a huge cleaning machine to get rid of any bits of cacao pulp and pieces of pod that may be stuck onto them. Then they're sorted by hand according to their quality, so that the chocolate-makers know exactly what mix of beans is going into their product.

Roasting the beans

To bring more of the chocolatey taste and smell out of the beans, they're roasted in huge ovens. Depending on the type of the beans and the type of chocolate being made, they can be roasted for 30 minutes to two hours, at temperatures of about 99-140°C (210-290°F).

For a strong-tasting chocolate, the beans are roasted for a short time on a high heat. Roasting them for a long time on a low heat produces a more delicate flavour.

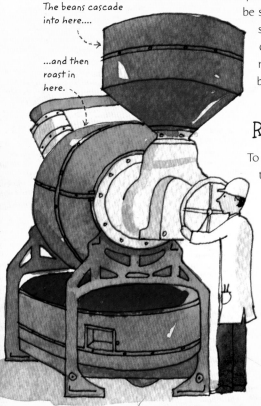

The beans cascade into here....

...and then roast in here.

Winnowing

Cacao beans are covered by thin shells, which have to be removed. This is the job of a winnowing machine. Inside this huge machine, metal cones crack the beans, then giant fans blow away the shells leaving broken pieces of cacao beans, called nibs. The nibs are taken to mills, where they are crushed between large grinding stones or heavy steel discs. The crushed nibs are then ground into a thick paste. No longer called cacao, the paste is known as cocoa liquor or cocoa mass.

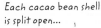
Each cacao bean shell is split open...

...and blown away...

...leaving crushed bean pieces called nibs...

...which are ground into cocoa mass.

A cup of cocoa

Some cocoa mass is made into cocoa powder. To do this, it's put in a press that squeezes the fat, called cocoa butter, out of it. This leaves a dry cake that is then ground into a powder, which is used in baking or for mixing with warm milk to make a drink.

Some gardeners spread cacao bean shells over their soil. The shells add nutrients to the soil as they rot, and keep the soil moist.

Cocoa powder, like this, is pure cocoa mass. Drinking chocolate powder is different because it contains added sugars and milk extracts.

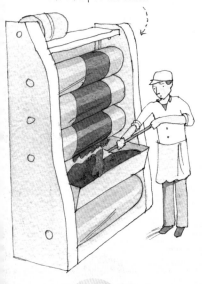

To make cocoa mass smoother, it's fed through rollers, set one on top of the other.

Adding ingredients

Most cocoa mass isn't made into powder but is used to make solid eating chocolate. To do this, chocolate-makers have to sweeten it and improve its texture, adding things such as sugar, vanilla and milk. The mixture is then pumped through a series of heavy rollers that grind it into a smooth paste.

Conching

The cocoa paste is run through a conching machine to refine its flavour and texture. The machine swirls and mixes the chocolate, using rollers that thrust back and forth through the mixture. To make the paste more creamy, cocoa butter is added. The bitter taste of the cacao slowly disappears and the chocolate that went into the machine gloopy or powdery, comes out thick and velvety.

Conching machines are so named because the first one — invented in 1879 — looked a little like a conch shell.

Early conching machines were open, so splashed chocolate about. Modern ones are covered.

Emulsifying

To break up even the tiniest lumps and bumps, some manufacturers pour their chocolate into a machine that works like an eggbeater, or they add an extract of soya beans to it. These processes are called emulsification.

Tempering and shaping

At the final stage, the liquid chocolate is tempered. This means it's stirred, cooled, and then slowly heated, over and over again until the look and feel of the chocolate are just right.

Tempering produces a glossy-looking chocolate that will melt smoothly in your mouth.

Tempered chocolate can be used as a liquid to flavour sweets, biscuits and ice creams, or squirted into moulds to be formed into shapes.

Chocolate can be made in a huge variety of sizes and shapes, from balls and bars, to eggs and rabbits.

Centres and fillings

In 1912, Belgian chocolate-maker, Jean Neuhaus, created the first bite-sized, filled chocolates. They contained cream and nougat.

In the early 1900s, new machines were invented that would make chocolates even more delicious. They could fill them with all kinds of centres, from brittle nuts and dried fruits, to whipped cream and chewy caramel.

Enrobing

To make hard-centred chocolates by hand, the fillings are dipped in melted chocolate. But large manufacturers use enrobing machines, which carry moulds on a conveyor line under a series of nozzles. The first nozzle squirts chocolate into the bottom of the mould, then a nut or fruit centre is placed on top. Another nozzle fills the mould with chocolate. Finally, the mould passes through a cooling tunnel to set.

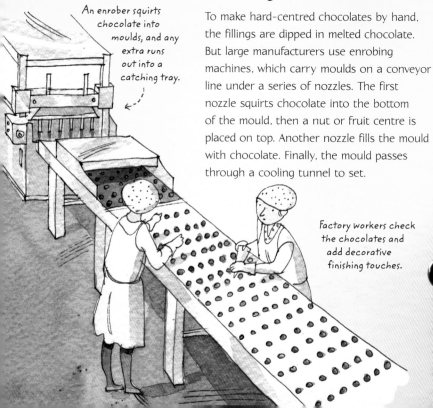

An enrober squirts chocolate into moulds, and any extra runs out into a catching tray.

Factory workers check the chocolates and add decorative finishing touches.

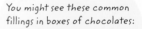

Here, a creamy filling is being piped into a chocolate-coated mould by hand.

Shell-moulding

Chocolates with soft centres are made by shell-moulding. Melted chocolate is poured into a mould, then most of it is tipped out. Some remains, coating the inside. When the mould is cooled, this coating solidifies, forming a shell. The soft centre is then squirted into a hole in the shell, and a layer of melted chocolate is laid over it, and cooled to seal in the filling.

Panning

To coat hard centres, such as nuts, in a thin layer of chocolate, some manufacturers use a chocolate version of a cement mixer, called a panner. The fillings roll around a rotating drum while being sprayed by a fine jet of liquid chocolate.

You might see these common fillings in boxes of chocolates:

- ◎ Nougat — whipped egg white, boiled sugar and honey, with almonds, nuts and fruit

- ◎ Truffle — a blend of chocolate, cocoa butter, sugar and powdered cream

- ◎ Praline — almonds and hazelnuts crushed finely and heated with sugar, then mixed with milk chocolate

- ◎ Creme fondant — sugar and glucose with added flavourings

The centres put into a panner have to be hard, like these nuts, to withstand all the tumbling about.

If something is described as chocolate-flavoured, it means that it contains up to around 5% cocoa solids. This isn't enough for it to be officially recognized as chocolate.

Types of chocolate

A chocolate's type depends on what it's made of, and how much of each ingredient it contains. The best way to know exactly what kind of chocolate you're looking at is to read the ingredients on the back of the packet, and see how much hardened cocoa mass – also known as cocoa solids – and sugar there is.

Unsweetened

Unsweetened chocolate – also called bitter chocolate, or baking chocolate in the USA – is just 100% cocoa solids, with no added ingredients. This is the richest and strongest chocolate you can buy. You probably wouldn't want to eat it on its own though, as it's extremely bitter and a little gritty.

The unsweetened chocolate in this chocolate roulade only tastes good because the recipe calls for it to be mixed with sugar and vanilla.

Bittersweet and semi-sweet

Also described as Continental or plain, this chocolate contains up to 75% cocoa solids, with a little added sugar and vanilla. Semi-sweet chocolate usually has more sugar and less cocoa solids than bittersweet, but there are no set rules.

This kind of chocolate could be labelled bittersweet by one chocolate-maker, but may be called semi-sweet by another.

Sweet

Sweet chocolate contains at least 15% cocoa solids. It is usually dark, like a sweeter version of bitter and semi-sweet chocolate, although some varieties have milk as an added ingredient. Sweet chocolate is mostly used in baking, but it can be eaten as it is.

Chefs use sweet chocolate when they want their food to taste very chocolatey, but without the bitterness of other types of chocolate used for cooking.

Sweet chocolate is also known as German chocolate. It's not from Germany, but is named after English chef Sam German, who, in 1852, invented sweet chocolate to be used for baking.

Dark

Dark chocolate means different things in different places. It can be of any level of sweetness but, generally, dark chocolate means bittersweet or semi-sweet. There's no upper limit to the amount of cocoa solids it can contain but, in the USA, it must be made of at least 35% cocoa solids and, in Europe, at least 45%.

Dark chocolate melts slowly and doesn't burn easily, so it is often used in dishes that need to be soft or runny, such as this chocolate sauce.

Milk

When making milk chocolate, manufacturers replace some of the cocoa solids with milk products, such as milk powder and cream, giving it a smoother, creamier texture. Milk chocolate should contain at least 12% milk. In the USA, it contains a minimum of 10% cocoa solids, and 25% in Europe.

Milk chocolate is sweeter than dark, and is the type most often used in chocolate bars and other confectionery.

Couverture

The word couverture means "covering" in French. Couverture chocolate is made with the highest quality cacao beans, and a high percentage of cocoa butter – between 30% and 40%. This produces a smooth, silky chocolate that melts easily. Couverture chocolate can be dark or milk.

Couverture chocolate's glossy look and intense flavour make it the chocolate covering of choice for chefs.

White

White chocolate doesn't contain any cocoa solids, so isn't really chocolate at all. It's made of at least 20% cocoa butter, and at least 14% milk solids, as well as sugar and vanilla.

In the USA, white chocolate can contain no more than 55% sugar, but in Europe there's no limit to the amount of sugar that can be added.

White chocolate is only white if it's made with vegetable fat. If it contains cocoa butter, it looks cream, like this.

Europe's finest

Since chocolate first arrived in Europe, the recipe has been adapted from country to country, with each region making its own versions. Some of the world's finest, highest-quality chocolate is now produced in Europe.

Belgian chocolate

Lots of chocolate in Belgium is still made by hand in small shops.

There are more than 2,000 chocolate shops dotted throughout Belgium – at least one in every town and village. Most Belgian chocolates are pralines which, in Belgium, means a chocolate case filled with any smooth, creamy filling. Belgian chocolate-makers pay particular attention to the look and design of the cases.

You can see the blend of white, milk and dark Belgian chocolate in these seashell-shaped pralines.

These Swiss truffles are soft, crumbly chocolates made with butter and cream.

Swiss chocolate

In Switzerland, chocolate is made with lots of cocoa butter and milk. The milk comes from Swiss cows that are raised on an organic diet of fresh grass and clover on mountain slopes. These fresh, rich ingredients make a super-smooth, creamy kind of chocolate.

Every year, the Swiss eat more than 9.5kg (21lbs) of chocolate per person. That's more than any other nationality.

French chocolate

French chocolate-lovers tend to prefer dark chocolate that is high in cocoa content and low in fat. In the best restaurants in France, specialist pastry chefs create chocolate desserts that are not only delicious, but also look like works of art.

French pastry chefs train for years to learn how to work with chocolate.

Many big shops and chain stores employ specialist chocolate tasters. Their job is to taste lots of different types of new chocolates and decide which ones will sell best.

Chocolate tasting

Tasting chocolate means more than just eating it – it's a way of detecting all the different flavours that come from the cacao beans and the added ingredients, such as sugar and vanilla. What the beans taste like depends on the type they are, where they're from, and which processes they've been through to be made into chocolate.

A clean start

To really taste a piece of chocolate it's a good idea to start with a completely clean palate, so there are no other tastes in your mouth. If you've just eaten something sweet, you won't be able to detect the sugariness of the chocolate and it may taste bitter. If you've just had something bitter, the chocolate may taste too sweet or weak in flavour.

To clean your palate before tasting chocolate, drink some warm water.

The more cocoa butter there is in a piece of chocolate, the less time it will take to melt in your mouth.

Warming up

Chocolate releases it flavours when it begins to melt in your mouth. To get it to reach melting point quickly, it's best to let it warm to room temperature before tasting it. Drinking warm water beforehand also helps you to get a more instant burst of flavour.

Milk chocolate should taste creamy and sweet.

Good quality chocolate should make a snapping sound when you break off a piece.

Slowly does it

After putting a piece of chocolate into your mouth, take your time and allow it to melt. This not only maximizes its flavours, but also lets you feel its texture. The melting chocolate should feel smooth, and not grainy or greasy. If it contains too much cocoa butter, the chocolate will coat the inside of your mouth as it melts. When you finally chew, do it slowly – enjoy every moment!

Cacao beans from different countries produce chocolate with distinct flavours:

- Brazil – subtle fruit tones
- Colombia – slightly bitter
- Trinidad – cinnamon
- Jamaica – hint of pineapple

Dark chocolate should have more intense flavours than milk chocolate. You might taste toasty, earthy tones with a little nuttiness.

Words for chocolate
in different languages:

- Spanish – Chocolate
  (chokko-lah-tay)

- French – Chocolat
  (sho-ko-la)

- Italian – Cioccolata
  (chokko-lata)

- Polish – Czekolada
  (cheko-lada)

- German – Schokolade
  (shoko-lada)

A world of chocolate

Chocolate is an important part of many people's lives all over the world. As well as being a huge, global business that provides millions of jobs on almost every continent, chocolate also plays a vital role in many different cultures and national celebrations around the world.

Africa

West Africa supplies around 70% of the world's cacao beans. The majority of West African plantations are small, family-run farms. Cacao is so valuable as an export that most of the farmers prefer to ship their beans to factories overseas rather than make it into chocolate to eat themselves. Eating or drinking chocolate is a treat for special occasions.

On many African cacao plantations, whole families work together to tend their cacao trees.

Central and South America

Cacao plantations still thrive in Central and South America, just as they did 3,000 years ago. Today, many of the cacao plantations are massive stretches of land run by big corporations. The locals here don't just grow chocolate, they eat it, too. Chocolate is used as a savoury ingredient in traditional recipes, blended with corn and chillies. Hot chocolate mixed with spices, such as pepper and cinnamon, is the national drink of Mexico.

In Mexico, the traditional way to froth up chocolate drinks is with a wooden frother, twisted between the palms of the hands.

The USA

Chocolate was first made in the USA in 1765, and is now a multi-million dollar business. Cacao doesn't grow in the USA, but the country is second only to the Netherlands as the biggest importer of cacao. It's also home to the world's largest chocolate factory, set up in Pennsylvania by Milton Hershey in 1894.

Chocolate-covered peanut butter cups were first made in the USA in the 1920s and are now one of the country's most popular snacks.

Spain

Chocolate has been part of Spanish culture ever since cacao beans were first brought to Spain in 1544. Traditional Spanish hot chocolate is a rich, sweet liquid so thick that it's more like a sauce than a drink, and is served in cafés and restaurants throughout the country. In the Spanish city of Barcelona there is a museum, and many shops and cafés, all dedicated to chocolate.

Hot chocolate served with sticks of fried dough is popular as a breakfast snack all over Spain.

In Austrian cafés, a cup of hot chocolate or coffee is often served with a chocolate-filled pastry.

Austria

Chocolate is part of daily life in Austria. All over the country, there are thousands of cafés and bakeries specializing in chocolate drinks, pastries and cakes. Vienna, the capital city, has its own form of hot chocolate which is thickened with heavy cream and egg yolk. Austria's love of chocolate is reflected in one of its most popular dishes, Sachertorte – a dense, doughy chocolate sponge cake, coated with dark chocolate.

Switzerland

Swiss chocolate-makers mould their products into many different shapes. Each season and region is associated with a different shape of chocolate. Chocolate chestnuts and mushrooms are made in autumn, and chocolate flowers signify the coming of spring. All year round, chocolate-makers in the different regions of Switzerland produce the local specialities. Jura, for example, is famous for its intricately designed watch-shaped chocolates.

Anyone who joins the Swiss army is given free army chocolate, which is wrapped in foil bearing the Swiss flag.

This chocolate cauldron filled with marzipan "vegetables" is a Genevan speciality.

In Zurich, shops sell chocolate models of a snowman-like figure made from straw. The straw man is burned as part of a festival celebrating the end of winter.

Chocolate-makers in Bern are known for creating models of bears — the city's mascot.

A little luxury

Like fashion houses, some luxury chocolate-makers launch different summer and winter ranges, plus special editions for Christmas and Easter.

Most chocolate products sold today are cheap snacks found in supermarkets or newsagents. But there is a growing demand for gourmet chocolates; freshly made, using only the finest ingredients. Increasingly, chocolatiers – chefs who specialize in making chocolates – are setting up their own, exclusive shops in towns and cities all over the world. The shops look like designer fashion boutiques, but sell only high-end confectioneries.

Best before

Many chocolatiers don't use any artificial preservatives in their products. Their focus is on developing the best aromas, flavours and textures, all of which may be tainted by adding preservatives. These luxury chocolates need to be eaten fresh – after two weeks, their aromas fade, their flavours weaken, and their textures change.

The chocolates are handled with care.

Gourmet chocolates need to be kept fresh, so shops usually display them in chilled cabinets and counters.

Luxury chocolates often come in expensive and attractive packaging.

Weird and wonderful

To make their chocolates special and different from any others on the market, many chocolatiers create distinctive-looking chocolates with original and often unusual flavours. The most expensive chocolates are covered in edible gold leaf or are delicately hand painted with floral designs.

Chocolate by post

Some chocolate boutiques have a chocolate subscription service to which customers sign up to be sent the latest chocolates every month. This is a good way for chocolatiers to advertise their new ranges and to get feedback on their creations from chocolate-lovers of all ages and backgrounds.

Here are some unusual flavours of chocolate available in gourmet chocolate shops:

 Lavender

Green tea

 Cola and almond

Marzipan and black olives

Goats' cheese and hazelnut

Fresh basil and sun-dried tomatoes

A chocolate future

Since people began making chocolate machines around 200 years ago, technology has played an important role in developing new types of chocolate. Today's food technicians are not only making new flavours of chocolate, but also inventing new forms of it.

Bendy chocolate

Solid chocolate bars have been the most popular form of chocolate ever since they were first made around 150 years ago. But, in the future, bars could be replaced by knots, plaits, curls, wiggles and swirls. These twisty shapes are now possible because a new form of elastic chocolate has been invented. It can be bent into any shape without having to be heated and without it losing its taste.

Elastic chocolate can be pushed through a nozzle to form a shape. The shape sets after half an hour.

A breath of fresh chocolate

For hundreds of years, the only ways to taste chocolate were to drink it or chew it. Now food scientists have invented a gadget that lets you inhale chocolate. Put the inhaler in your mouth, breathe in, and tiny particles of chocolate come shooting out, landing directly onto the parts of your mouth where your tastebuds are. This gives a more intense tasting experience than simply eating or drinking chocolate.

Fruit-covered chocolate

Fruit and chocolate can make a delicious combination, and the easiest way to mix the two flavours is to dip fruit into melted chocolate. But now scientists have found a way to insert chocolate inside the fruit. They do this by freeze-drying the fruit to remove the water, and then injecting the chocolate into the spaces left behind.

The cars of the future could run on cocoa butter. The butter extracted from cacao beans can be made into biodiesel, which fuels vehicles. In 2007, two British adventurers travelled from England to Mali, West Africa, in a truck powered entirely by cocoa biodiesel.

A chocolate-infused strawberry looks like a normal strawberry on the outside, but bite into it and you'll taste the strands of chocolate in its fibres.

At the end of 1899, Queen Victoria sent a tin of chocolates bearing her portrait as a New Year gift to each of the 40,000 British soldiers fighting in the Boer War in South Africa.

Chocolate celebration

Chocolate plays an important part in cultural festivities and religious holidays all over the world. In many cultures, it's traditional to celebrate special occasions by giving gifts of chocolate.

Eggs at Easter

The crocodile-style pattern you can see on this Easter egg emerged in Germany as a way of disguising any imperfections in the egg's surface.

The Christian festival of Easter celebrates new life and the rising of Jesus Christ from the dead. Eggs were traditionally given at this time to symbolize rebirth. In the 1800s, chocolate Easter eggs began to be produced in Germany and France, and they quickly replaced real eggs as the most popular Easter gift. The first chocolate eggs were solid but, soon after, hollow eggs were made, which could be filled with sweets and toys.

These foil-wrapped chocolates look like the brightly painted eggs that were traditionally given at Easter time.

The Day of the Dead

In Mexico, a festival of remembrance, called The Day of the Dead, is held in November. Families visit the graves of their ancestors and give each other gifts of chocolate skulls. This originates from ancient times, when Mexican nobles were buried with cups filled with chocolate, to keep them fed on their journey to the afterlife.

On The Day of the Dead, children decorate chocolate skulls with brightly coloured icing, like this.

In Japan, women give chocolate to their work colleagues as well as their loved-ones on Valentine's Day.

A month later...

Sweet Valentines

In 1861, English chocolatier Richard Cadbury created the first ever Valentine's chocolates. Since then, the practice of giving chocolate on Valentine's Day has spread throughout the world. In Japan, women give chocolates to men on the 14th February then, a month later, the men have to give a more expensive chocolate gift in return.

A savoury ingredier

Sweet chocolate is a relatively modern invention – for over 2,000 years, people only thought of chocolate as savoury. The ancient form of savoury chocolate is still used today. Cooks around the world have found that good quality dark chocolate gives a thick, silky texture and a sharp tang to meaty and spicy dishes.

Holy mole

According to legend, chocolate was first added to meat by Mexican nuns in the 16th century. Asked by their bishop to create a special dish for an important guest, the nuns prayed for inspiration, then gathered over 20 ingredients to blend into a sauce for a turkey stew. One of these ingredients was chocolate. The resulting sauce, called mole (pronounced "mo-lay"), was a huge success and eventually the stew became Mexico's national dish.

In France, chocolate is used in red wine sauces.

In Spain, chocolate is added to meaty dishes such as calf's tongue and lobster.

In Italy, chocolate is used to flavour pasta and sweet-and-sour sauces, and in rabbit stews.

In South Africa, chocolate is added to game dishes, such as pigeon and guinea fowl, and to sauces served with beef fillet.

This savoury chocolate sauce is called Mole Poblano, named after the Mexican city of Puebla where it was first made.

The grated chocolate that's been sprinkled on top of this chilli con carne brings out the flavour of the meat.

Chocolate chilli

In 1922, American hot dog stand owner, Tom Kiradjieff, invented a chocolate dish that combined elements from a Greek stew and Texan beef chilli. The new dish became known as Cincinnati chilli, named after the city where it was first made. Today, the chilli is served in around 200 chilli parlours throughout Cincinnati.

Nibbling on nibs

Pieces of roasted cacao beans, called cacao nibs, can be eaten raw or cooked in sauces for savoury dishes. They have a bittersweet, roasted flavour and a crunchy texture.

Cacao nibs can be put in a pepper grinder and sprinkled over pastas and salads.

Healthy chocolate

Most people wouldn't think that nibbling on chocolate could ever be healthy, but eating the right kind of chocolate in moderation can be good for you. There are over 300 natural chemicals in chocolate, and scientists are constantly discovering new information about their beneficial effects on the human body.

Some traditional healers in Latin America still use chocolate as medicine, just as their ancient ancestors did. Chocolate is rubbed onto bee and scorpion stings, and drunk to help cure kidney infections, diarrhoea and bronchitis.

Eating one or two squares of dark chocolate, like this, every day may help to keep your heart healthy.

A happy heart

Scientific research shows that some kinds of chocolate can be good for your heart. Those that contain a high percentage of cocoa solids have lots of antioxidants. These help fight off heart disease by preventing damage to your body cells or by repairing damage that has already been done.

Chocolate that contains cocoa butter and no other types of fat may increase your body's levels of good cholesterol. This cleans the walls of the blood vessels around your heart.

Dark vs. milk

The higher the chocolate's cocoa content, the better it is for you. Dark chocolate is healthier than milk chocolate because the milk varieties contain fewer cocoa solids, as well as more calories and more saturated fat. A single bar of dark chocolate also contains about three times as many antioxidants as a bar of milk chocolate.

Cacao beans are one of the richest sources of magnesium of any food. Magnesium is a mineral which gives you energy, is good for blood pressure, builds strong bones, strengthens muscles and helps prevent migraines.

It takes 12 cacao beans to make 28g (1oz) of dark chocolate...

... but only four beans to make the same amount of milk chocolate.

Brain boost

Some of the chemicals in cacao – such as theobromine and anandamide – have been found to help people stay alert and happy. They stimulate the brain, dull pain, act as a natural anti-depressant and can even put someone in a good mood.

Scientists have also found that some types of chemicals found in cacao, called flavanols, may increase blood flow to the brain, which can help to improve memory.

Research has shown that even just smelling chocolate can relax you and put you in a daydreamy frame of mind.

Chocolate art

Chocolate can be melted, moulded, piped and set, changing form and shape. It's no wonder then, that many people see chocolate not just as food, but also as a medium for creating striking pieces of art.

It takes great skill to create delicate shapes and intricate detailing in chocolate, like this.

Scrumptious sculptures

Chocolate sculptures may not be as durable as ones made from stone or metal, but they are popular centrepieces for special occasions, particularly when they can later be eaten by the guests. In Europe, some chocolatiers display chocolate sculptures in detailed scenes in the windows of their shops.

Themed shop window displays can draw in the crowds.

There's a whole range of products for sale made out of chocolate, including:

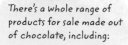

- ◎ Shoes
- ◎ Jewellery
- ◎ Games, like chess and draughts
- ◎ Tea sets
- ◎ Flowers
- ◎ Place names
- ◎ Lifesize rooms, with chocolate decor and furniture

This melted chocolate is being piped in elaborate patterns drawn on baking parchment. When they set, they'll be scraped off and used to decorate cakes.

Edible paintings

Melted chocolate dries and hardens in a similar way to paint, so some people use it to create edible portraits, landscapes and still-life pictures. Companies sometimes commission chocolate versions of their logos as a way of promoting their brands.

Some chocolate paintings come with frames which are also made out of chocolate, dusted with edible gold or silver.

Food as fashion

New York and Paris host annual chocolate exhibitions, during which chocolate fashion shows are held. For these glitzy events, designers and chocolatiers join forces to create stunning collections of chocolate dresses. Some of the dresses are made from "chocolate leather" – a combination of chocolate and corn syrup.

"Chocolate leather" behaves just like a fabric, enabling the designers to cut out the dress shapes easily.

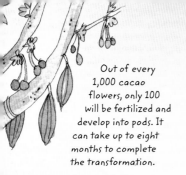

Out of every 1,000 cacao flowers, only 100 will be fertilized and develop into pods. It can take up to eight months to complete the transformation.

The top five countries that consume the most chocolate per person are:
◎ Switzerland
◎ Austria
◎ Ireland
◎ Germany
◎ Norway

Cocoa butter is not only used to make chocolate, but it's also used in cosmetics.

Chocolate cravings can't be satisfied by any other sweet food.

Amazing but true

Here are some surprising and extraordinary facts that you may not know about chocolate.

Growing together

Cacao flowers and fruit grow directly from the trunks of cacao trees. The trees are in flower and in fruit all year round, so you can see blossoms and pods on the trunks at the same time.

Surviving the blast

The Trinitario type of cacao bean only exists because of a mysterious natural disaster in Trinidad. Records from 1727 state that a "blast" destroyed most of the cacao trees on the island, forcing the growers to cross-breed the remaining few to make an entirely new species. No one knows what the word "blast" means – it could be referring to a hurricane, drought or fungal disease epidemic.

Crazy cravings

Chocolate is the most commonly craved food. More than twice the number of women as men experience chocolate cravings.

Chocolate downpour

The world's largest chocolate fountain is in The Bellagio Hotel in Las Vegas, USA. It's over 7m (26ft) tall and holds nearly two tonnes of chocolate, which is heated and circulated by an elaborate under-floor system of pipes, pumps and valves.

There are three chocolate rivers in this fountain at The Bellagio: one dark, one milk and one white.

Chocohotel

The Italian town of Perugia is home to the world's first hotel dedicated entirely to chocolate. Its three floors are named Milk, Dark and Gianduja (a hazelnut chocolate), and guests are given a bar of chocolate with their room key. The hotel has a huge chocolate shop and a restaurant offering an All-Cacao Menu – every dish on it contains cacao.

On average, people eat more chocolate during winter than in any other season.

Ingredients:

⊙ Makes about 12 slices

- 150g (5oz) self-raising flour
- 50g (2oz) cocoa powder
- 2 teaspoons baking powder
- 200g (7oz) butter, softened
- 200g (7oz) soft brown sugar
- 1½ teaspoons vanilla essence
- 4 large eggs
- 150g (5oz) dark chocolate
- 150ml (¼ pint) double cream

⊙ You will also need a 20cm (8in) round cake tin.

Rich chocolate cake

This deliciously sticky cake is covered with a thick, creamy topping, called a ganache. The ganache and the amount of cocoa powder in the sponge give the cake a very intense, chocolatey taste, so it's best to serve it in thin slices. Dark, moist chocolate cakes like this one are popular throughout Europe.

1. Heat the oven to 180°C, 350°F, gas mark 4. Put the tin onto a piece of baking parchment and draw around it with a pencil. Cut out the circle, just inside the line.

2. Use a paper towel to wipe a little cooking oil over the insides of the tin and put the paper circle into the tin. Sift the flour, cocoa and baking powder into a large bowl.

3. Put the butter and sugar into another bowl and beat them together with a spoon until they are light and fluffy. Add the vanilla and beat the mixture again.

4. Crack one egg into a cup. Add it to the butter mixture with one tablespoon of the flour mixture. Beat it well. Then, repeat this step with each of the remaining eggs.

5. Add the rest of the flour mixture and stir it in gently, moving the spoon in the shape of a number eight. Pour the chocolatey mixture into the cake tin.

Take the paper off the bottom.

6. Level the top with the back of a spoon. Bake the cake for 40-45 minutes, then poke a skewer into it. If cake mixture sticks to it, bake the cake for ten minutes more.

7. When the skewer comes out clean, the cake is cooked. Leave the cake in the tin for a few minutes, then hold the tin upside down over a wire rack and gently shake it out.

8. To make the ganache, break the chocolate into a heatproof bowl and add the cream. Then, pour about 5cm (2in) water into a pan and heat it.

9. When the water bubbles, take the pan off the heat. Carefully, put the bowl into the pan. Stir the chocolate until it melts. Let the ganache cool, then put it into the fridge.

◉ This cake is best eaten the day you make it.

Find out how to make chocolate curls on page 57.

10. Wait until the cake is completely cold and the ganache is like soft butter. Then, spread the ganache over the top and sides of the cake.

Choc-chip brownies

Ingredients:

◉ Makes 9 squares

- 200g (7oz) plain chocolate
- 2 large eggs
- 125g (5oz) butter, softened
- 275g (10oz) caster sugar
- ½ teaspoon vanilla essence
- 50g (2oz) self-raising flour
- 25g (1oz) plain flour
- 2 tablespoons cocoa powder
- 100g (4oz) walnut or pecan pieces

◉ You will also need a 20cm (8in) square cake tin.

Brownies were first made in the USA over 100 years ago and are still one of the most popular cakes in America today. This double-chocolate recipe is especially for chocolate lovers. Bite through the brownie's thin chocolatey crust, and you'll discover chewy chunks of chocolate in the delightfully squidgy middle.

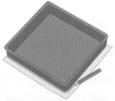

1. Heat the oven to 180°C, 350°F, gas mark 4. Put the tin onto a piece of baking parchment. Draw around it and cut out the shape.

2. Use a paper towel to wipe a little cooking oil over the insides of the tin and put the paper square into the tin. Heat 5cm (2in) water in a pan.

3. When the water bubbles, take the pan off the heat. Break half of the chocolate into a heatproof bowl and put the bowl into the pan.

4. Stir the chocolate until it melts, then take the bowl out of the pan. Break the eggs into a small bowl and beat them with a fork.

5. Beat the butter, sugar and vanilla in another bowl until they're fluffy. Add the eggs, a little at a time, beating them after each addition.

6. Sift both types of flour and the cocoa powder into the bowl. Then, add the melted chocolate and mix it all together.

7. Break the rest of the chocolate into small chunks. Stir them, and the nuts, into the mixture, then spoon it into the tin. Smooth the top.

8. Bake the brownies for 35 minutes. They're ready when they have risen slightly and a crust has formed on top. They will still be soft inside.

⊘ You can store these brownies for up to three days in an airtight container.

9. Leave the brownies in the tin for 20 minutes to cool, then cut them into squares. They are delicious eaten while still slightly warm.

Chocolate mousse

There are many variations of chocolate mousse.
The dessert can vary in texture from a light,
frothy foam to a thick, dreamy goo. This recipe
makes a luxuriously creamy mousse that's best
served straight from the fridge.

☉ This mousse is best eaten
the day you make it.

Sprinkle curls of
chocolate over
the mousse.

You could
decorate your
mousse with
mint leaves.

1. Heat about 5cm (2in) of water in a pan. When the water bubbles, turn off the heat. Break the chocolate into a heatproof bowl.

2. Add four tablespoons of the cream to the chocolate pieces. Then, put the bowl into the pan and leave it for a minute or two.

3. Stir the mixture until the chocolate melts. Then, carefully lift the bowl out of the pan and leave it to cool for ten minutes.

4. Pour the rest of the cream into a large bowl. Whisk it quickly until it thickens and forms peaks when you lift up the whisk.

5. Stir a spoonful of the cream into the chocolate. Stir in the rest with a metal spoon, moving the spoon in the shape of a number eight.

6. Spoon the mousse into four glasses or bowls. Put them in the fridge for at least an hour to chill before you eat them.

Chocolate curls

1. To make little curls, use a vegetable peeler to scrape chocolate from the edges of a chocolate bar.

2. For bigger curls, scrape the peeler down the back of the chocolate bar. Keep scraping to make more curls.

You may find that the dark chocolate version of this mousse tastes more like milk chocolate than you expected. This is because adding cream takes away some of the chocolate's bitterness.

Triple chocolate cookie.

Ingredients:

◉ Makes 24 cookies

- 75g (3oz) butter, softened
- 75g (3oz) caster sugar
- 75g (3oz) soft light brown sugar
- 1 medium egg
- 1 teaspoon vanilla essence
- 150g (5oz) plain flour
- 4 tablespoons cocoa powder
- 1/2 teaspoon baking powder
- 100g (4oz) milk chocolate
- 100g (4oz) white chocolate

This is the ultimate cookie recipe for chocoholics, as it uses two types of chocolate chunks in a chocolate dough. Cookies made with this method are also known as drop cookies because the dough is dropped from a spoon onto the baking tray.

◉ Keep the cookies in an airtight container and eat them within five days.

1. Heat the oven to 180°C, 350°F, gas mark 4. Use a paper towel to wipe a little oil over two baking trays. Put the butter into a bowl.

2. Stir both types of sugar into the butter until the mixture is smooth and creamy. Break the egg into a small bowl and beat it.

3. Mix the vanilla essence into the egg. Add the eggy liquid to the buttery mixture a little at a time, stirring it well between each addition.

4. Sift the flour, cocoa and baking powder into the bowl. Stir until smooth. Break the chocolate into small chunks and add them to the bowl.

5. Drop a heaped teaspoonful of the mixture onto a tray. Add more dollops, spacing them out well, then flatten them with the back of a fork.

6. Put the cookies in the oven and bake them for ten minutes, until they are firm on top. Then, carefully take the trays out of the oven.

7. Leave the cookies on the trays for a few minutes. Use a spatula to lift them onto a wire rack and leave them to cool.

Chocolate chip cookies were first made in 1930 by an American innkeeper. While making chocolate cookies for her guests one day, she realized she had run out of cooking chocolate. Instead, she decided to add small chunks of a chocolate bar to the cookie dough.

Ingredients:

◎ Makes 2 servings

- 100g (4oz) plain chocolate
- 2 teaspoons caster sugar
- A few drops of vanilla extract
- A pinch of ground cinnamon
- A tiny pinch of chilli flakes
- 450ml (3/4 pint) milk

◎ Topping options:
- 75 ml (3fl oz) of whipping cream
- A bar of plain or milk chocolate
- A small handful of mini marshmallows or chunks of fudge

Chilli hot chocolate

In Mexico, people drink hot chocolate mixed with chilli, just as the ancient Mexicans did thousands of years ago. This recipe shows you how to make Mexican hot chocolate and then gives you options for different tempting toppings.

1. Break the chocolate into a small saucepan. Add the sugar, vanilla, cinnamon, chilli and milk. Then, heat it gently, stirring all the time.

2. When the chocolate has melted, beat the mixture with a whisk until it starts to boil and is very smooth and frothy.

Stop when the cream makes soft peaks, like this.

3. Take the pan off the heat. Then, carefully pour the hot chocolate through a small strainer into two mugs.

For a whipped cream topping, pour the cream into a bowl before you make the chocolate. Whisk the cream quickly until it thickens.

For grated chocolate, put the chocolate bar into the freezer for a few minutes until it's really hard. Grate it over the top of your drink.

A pinch is the amount you can pick up between your first finger and your thumb. Use a really tiny pinch for the chilli, or the hot chocolate might taste too spicy. You can use chilli powder instead if you like — then you won't need to strain the hot chocolate in step 3.

You can find out how to make a cookie to go with your drink on page 58.

You could sprinkle a few mini marshmallows over the top of your finished drink.

Chocolate cupcakes

These moist, fudge-topped cupcakes don't contain any wheat, gluten, dairy products or nuts, so are a good choice if you're allergic to any of these things. If you are, make sure that the particular brand of dairy-free spread, chocolate and cocoa you choose doesn't contain an ingredient you're allergic to.

Ingredients:

⊙ Makes 12 large cupcakes

- 175g (6oz) dairy-free spread
- 175g (6oz) caster sugar
- 3 medium eggs
- 40g (1½oz) cocoa powder
- 125g (4½oz) fine polenta (cornmeal)
- 1½ teaspoons gluten-free baking powder
- 1 teaspoon vanilla essence

⊙ For the chocolate fudge topping:
- 150g (5oz) plain chocolate
- 75g (3oz) dairy-free spread
- 75g (3oz) icing sugar

⊙ You will also need a 12-hole muffin tray and 12 paper muffin cases.

Beat the mixture until it's pale and fluffy.

1. Heat the oven to 190°C, 375°F, gas mark 5. Put a paper case into each hole of the muffin tray. Beat the dairy-free spread and sugar together in a bowl.

2. Break the eggs into a small bowl and beat them with a fork. Add the eggs to the buttery mixture a little at a time, beating it well after each addition.

 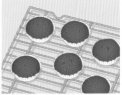

3. Add the cocoa, polenta, baking powder, vanilla and a tablespoon of water to the bowl and mix well. Spoon the mixture into the cases. Bake the cupcakes for 20 minutes.

4. When the cupcakes have risen and are firm on top, take them out of the oven. After five minutes, put them on a wire rack to cool. Meanwhile, make the fudge topping.

6 Without the fruit, you can store the cakes for up to five days in an airtight container.

Berries make a decorative finishing touch.

Raspberry

Redcurrant

Blueberry

5. Break the chocolate into a heatproof bowl with the dairy-free spread. Heat about 5cm (2in) water in a pan until the water bubbles. Take the pan off the heat.

6. Put the bowl into the pan and wait until everything has melted. Then, wearing oven gloves, take the bowl out of the pan and sift the icing sugar into the bowl.

7. Stir everything until it is thoroughly mixed. When the cakes are cool, spoon on the topping and leave it to set (this takes around 30 minutes).

INDEX

ACKNOWLEDGEMENTS

Cover designed by Karen Tomlins

Additional illustrations by Molly Sage

Recipes by Catherine Atkinson

Recipe photography by Howard Allman

With thanks to Abigail Wheatley and Victoria Richards

PHOTO CREDITS